I0091152

minjerribah

Also by Madeleine Onraet

The Heart's Curtain

minjerribah

poems

MADELEINE ONRAET

Insight Poetry

First published in 2022 by Insight Poetry

Copyright © Madeleine Onraet 2022
Visit: www.madeleineonraet.com

All rights reserved.

No part of this publication may be reproduced, stored in a retrieval system, or transmitted, in any form or by any means, electronic, mechanical, photocopying, recording or otherwise without the prior written permission of the publisher.

ISBN (paperback) 978-0-6453474-0-1
ISBN (ebook) 978-0-6453474-1-8

In gratitude of the land
and for Steve, Tom and Harry

Acknowledgment of the Quandamooka People and Country

We acknowledge the Quandamooka People, Traditional Owners and Custodians of the sacred land of Minjerribah. We respect their deep spiritual connection to Country and honour Elders past, present and emerging, whose wisdom have ensured the continuation of culture and traditional practices here for over 21,000 years.

Contents

We carry place
within.

Introduction

My family moved to the bayside Brisbane suburb of Wynnum North when I was five years old. Our house was nestled into the side of a hill overlooking the Quandamooka waters of Moreton Bay. Each morning, we woke to see the silent beauty of Minjerribah in the distance. We visited the island on day trips and holidays.

In my twenties, I married and travelled overseas. We returned to Minjerribah after the birth of our eldest son and were again impacted by the land's presence. Annual visits to the island became a sacred part of our young family's rhythm. Our sons are now young men and we continue our retreats at Minjerribah.

This book is a selection of poems written over more than twenty years. They express a personal response to the beauty and wisdom of this land.

May we together respect the land on which we walk.

ARRIVE

We arrive this time

to find the waves
   reach halfway up the beach
      to touch the still lagoon
   and press their sea salt lips
into the tea leaf stain

of stagnant pool,
   the trees
      in white trunks stand
   like ancestors
around the edge

winnowing
   with their grey
      and thoughtful sticks.
   The waves
roll the dream, loosening

the silt within.
   Everything returns
      through ebb
   and flow.

Everything returns in the end.

LESSONS

My youngest son throws his body at the sand.
In the movement, such abandon.

I stand watchful at the top
of our morning sand dune.

Do I enter life like that?

Out to sea, a school of dolphins
leaps the waves.

My son tumbles,
laughing at the bottom of the dune.

A forty-something woman
throws her body to the wind.

bird upturned
in orange flower –
we greet the sun.

GOANNA

On Minjerribah,
in kookaburra time,
we sat down
beside the nutbrown
cones of swamp
bottlebrush

listening.

Ears can be eyes
and eyes, ears.
Feet can be brain
and brain, feet.

Do not forget
these things –
they're in you.

Goanna knows,
padding through the forest
like a queen.

Goanna knows.

GREAT EGRET

A
fine
white
line

standing guard on our roof

arrests
me
with the beauty
of her slenderness.

Some creatures
graced
to touch
a cloud.

My deep
respect
for her
incisiveness

her watchful eye.

REFLECTIONS

Orange umbrella
holds
a woman
walking
.... on .... the .... wet .... sand ....
walking
woman
holds
orange umbrella.

Shell

home
or grave?

in the corner
of my eye

seagull
waits.

THERE IS NOT A CLOUD IN THE SKY

"I want to be
so intimate
with you,"
my husband says.

Our children play along the water's edge
rippling light
like stars.

Sea folding

Being together
suddenly like this
at the end of a year
beside the sea.

We fold
into companionship
conscious
of the family
we are.

Our need of nourishing,
our need of rest,
and space and place
to know each other
as we grow.

The sustenance
of this.

Kookaburra

To wake with kookaburra
tumbling laughter
to my pillow
on a fresh
gust

of sea –

I am reborn.

After lunch

He: I am going to draw a line in the sand about it.

She: Good luck with that – the tide comes in.

Brother and sister

Feet traverse headland rock
   with an ease
grown in childhoods
   formed by sea
and sky and sand.

Brother and sister
   carrying boards; he tilts
his head towards her
   with a zinc smile.

He slightly takes the lead
   but it is she
he leans into
   in their liquidity

of walk past the pandanus palms
   through
warm morning air.

They move as beach,
   as cloud,
tide drifting through a wave,

they slide into the sea
  over the break
as one.

Shell ii

waves
   waves
waves

polishing

ALONE

That day I walked the beach alone,
I knew the sages
within their weathered mountain huts.

Allow alone and existence
penetrates
the heart.

We are brought close –
closeness
opening
through the body

as a thousand flowerings
of happiness.

Do you remember that September?

We were cooped
up indoors
for days. The wind
rushed at us
from the north
to agitate the waves
and splash
our windowpanes.

"The wind – the wind,"
you said,
and paced the floor
like a wounded animal
in need of movement
and of space.

"The wind, the wind,"
you said.

"Daddy, will you please
colour in," said Tom,
eyes wide
and clear
in the early morning
light.

Each night we dreamed
while you tossed and turned
as the wind
taunted you
with its whistling.

We slept,
the child in my womb
in the belly of a sea,
and Tom beside me.

On the seventh day,
you woke.

"The wind is gone!"
you cried,

released
onto the sand
to run

with Tom
light-stepping over
shells to follow you.

Slowly then, I walked. Sun shone
warm
upon my skin

and everything was still

as hundreds

    thousands... of tiny, yellow butterflies

      lifted into air.

with an eye
open to the stars
dolphin sleeps.

GENERATIONAL

Seeing her stop, bend low, pick up the stick
to write in the sand
she seems so young,
almost seventy, yet just a child
her long-sleeved shirt
fluttering blue
in the breeze.

She writes so slow, as though
there is nothing now for her
to do in these moments on a beach,
her grandsons
floating around her like clouds.

We seek to clarify ourselves in words,
I think.
To distil that something more –

And it is good. It's good
to lean towards the sand,
to let the wind rush through
the length
and breadth of who we think
we are.

I watch my mother write,
marvelling that once it was the other
way and she watched me
pen magic in the sand
though tragically, I do not think she did,
which became in part
the problem,
when parents do not see
our messages.

Waves roll,

hear them roar,
then draw in close
to see her word

written
for us all –

Éternité

Raindrops

Raindrops
on a table
on a balcony
by the sea.

Do I abandon?

A poet knows,
her heart
asks she live
her part.

As was known
by the first
poem
ever journeying

through human
soul.
Leave no trace.
Let footprints
vanish.

May I serve the rain,
table,
balcony
and sea.

May I meet them,
knowing nothing.

After a night of rain, the sea

is melodious with calm. I too, know God
within her opening, like the soft
lining of a whale,
this touch of sheets. My body
sensing textures of the soul
in your innocence

of sleep.
I press my leg
into your side, into my wondering
at what it means when life
is here unfurled like wild sea flowers

and everything is still.
Earth's silence
is embedded.

beach primrose
still holding the dune
at dusk.

Water's edge

"I would say it's gloriously imperfect,"
　I declare

to wind
　and waves
their wash enveloping
　our quickening
toes

as we retreat
　exhale

clean as whistling shells.

We think we can control,
　I muse,

footprints
　in the sand.

Home Beach

Fish can fly!
I cry

at death
as an ascending

swift portal
out of sea.

And we are chosen.
Eagle knows.

FAMILY WALK TO KARBOORA

Through thick humid
stillness
cut by scribbly gum
and banksia pine
brushed
by cool
fern

we walk
aware of

quiet

so loud
in technological
teenage ears.

I feel the land
pull deep

feel her
through my feet.

DUSK CLOUD

Dusk cloud comes so close
to where we sit
on the deck, I can reach
for her, can wrap her
round me like a soft

blanket of desire,
a wish,
a remembering.

Delight in being here
to hold the loveliness
of sky
in my arms.

HOME

In deep night,
the softness
of your body
brings me home
into myself.

Authenticity is a gift
we share.

It is the strongest
life of us.

The positioning of shells

Wet sand
becomes brown
rock
we climb

towards sky.
Our ascent
as seamless
as the tide's turn

below
marked by
the line of shells.
Your steadiness

as you choose
deliberately
to make your
own way

I understand
how each wave
can feel a need
to chart its course.

But the sight
of your black-bucket hat
so near the top
before me

is dredging wide my heart

eleven
is so young
to sail alone.

COUNTERPOINT

After lunch, we rest.
Our children settle,
stretched out on the floor.

Suddenly, you say:

"The older I become,
the more I'm struck
by a fragility.

A child swims,
I am alert to sharks,
strong currents,
a towering wave."

I turn
in counterpoint
as I so often do.

"Tenacity," I say.

"The pot plant
that you cut
and nearly
threw away.

Have you seen
its shoots?"

North Gorge

Turtle
rises
from
the
depths

as I lean like a she-oak from
the gorge rock
above.

Who can say
why anything happens?
Why anything matters
at all?

As my eyes scour turquoise waters
turtle

meets
me
at the intersecting point of
wave
wind
sun
joy

What does she teach me?

Turtle teaches
in all things
is dignity.

In dignity
resides
all things.

empty chair

late afternoon
  and an empty chair

by the water's
  rippling edge.

nearby a man
  and two boys

hold fishing
  lines.

silence
  takes the sky

and pulls it through
  our fingertips

everything is here
  as sea.

MINJERRIBAH SUNSET

It is the emptiness
    of trees,
and the promise
    of sky.

Already I am
    through the portal
of the whale's dark
    eye

vanished.

When the sacred lights
    ascend
in fluke migration
    from the south

I will have gone from you

    fully Here.

        The mystery
            of light's ancient
                fires

                night becoming.

Brahminy kite

Wings penetrate sky

like fish
know
sea –
wet
with
wonderment.

Below

Sea moves with mystery today.
Grey with mist, its tone is low.
Waves shift with sullenness
like an adolescent boy
who's filled with strange power
he does not yet identify
to be his own,
and so it lurks
beneath the contours of this world
to ask, what exactly is it here
that churns the loins,
pulsates the flesh,
veils a tenderness
of heart
with first bewilderments.

The sea moves –
the secret of its force
ten thousand leagues
below.

Amity

After storm, the bay is clear.

Trawlers shelter in the shallows
    and the children play
by the shore.

It's simple – and life was made
    as this

this substance we can catch
    that's slipping.

Night Journey

My son's sadness has a beauty

Adolescence is a strange ocean
  of becoming real. These makings of the pearl,
our journeying in how to be
  in a lost world.

His soul a shimmering, a sunset lit

  by storm, the silence of the whale,
awoken by the melancholy of the night

in sea breeze
  adrift through darkness.

FATHER AND SON

Would you
like to be
a wave
or cloud?

A wave.
And you?

I would
like to be
a cloud.

Horizon smiles –
sky skims sea.

Coastal

Beneath the broadbrush strokes
   of a surfacing we know,
there is an interior
   that shifts

with sands sculpted into
   shapes
we might not recognise
   as being our own.

For who are we
   beneath the cloaks of trees
and smiles
   and blossom, and the whale's tail
glimpsed

 in joy?

We are the movements of the tide,
   a change in wind,
a melt
   in sun ineffable

drawing all
   in circular return

to know ourselves – clear waters
    rushing through our lives,
poured from skies
    of new beginnings possible
as night

    sweated in dream
and by anxiety
    and loss.

To let our clothes fall,
    return to ocean

 a secret
    slid from shell.

DUNWICH CEMETERY

As I walk amongst the trees,
peace finds me. It is in the breeze
and in the glimpse of bay
and in this sense of land
I feel to be receiving me
with an immensity

of calm.

Strange, how wandering near graves
can heal our wounds. Grief meets grief
and finds a personhood
of shared understanding

only suffering can bring.

Trees bathe me with their gentleness
and earth holds firm
in her commitment
to the wholeness that we are

when we are walking right

and listening. That's all we need.
Become the listening

and dignity remains
as it has always been
within our bones
as storylines,

the story of a heart
  gone, gone, gone
    as love.

Shell III

I see the nakedness
of shell
in sand.

I do not
take her.

I bow
with her
into the deep want
of sea.

The leaving

It's the leaving that's so sad.

As if the emptiness
reveals a reality
we so long
to forget.

A family arrives next door –

excited shouts, bright flowers
in a clear house. And like the snap
of twig underfoot,

we know that we must leave.

Our exit decreed
by the fine line of birds
in flight
towards the west.

They form our heralding

our slow becoming something
new
once again.

RETURN

We are to leave –
and so I find I reach,
seek something
I can take.

But then I hear the sea,
recall the bird's clear eye,
the wings of butterflies
in wattle
flowers.

What can I take
that is not already here
in my heart?

What is my seeking
but forgetting
everything
the land
has taught.

Light suffuses me.

Dolphin leaps
and everything is giving
of itself
into the land's
deep calm.

All I ever know
is what is always
here

releasing me.

Notes

Minjerribah is located on the eastern edge of Moreton Bay near Brisbane, Queensland. It is the world's second largest sand island. The Quandamooka people have lived here for over 21,000 years. It was named Stradbroke Island in 1827 by British naval officer Captain Henry Rous after his father, the Earl of Stradbroke. The island has also become affectionately known as "Straddie".

Great egret: The eastern great egret is a snowy-white wetland bird often seen on Minjerribah.

Raindrops: This poem is in part a response to the statement by Leonardo da Vinci that "Art is never finished, only abandoned".

Beach primrose: Beach evening primrose has single, soft-yellow flowers that open early and last only a few hours.

Family walk to Karboora: Karboora is the Quandamooka name for Blue Lake.

North Gorge: Bay and ocean waters around Minjerribah have six of the world's seven species of marine turtle. Loggerhead turtles and, more rarely, green turtles nest here. Both are endangered species. Leatherbacks are seen infrequently in these waters.

Brahminy kite: The brahminy kite is one of four raptors (birds of prey) seen on Minjerribah. It has a reddish-brown back and wings, with a white head.

Amity: Amity Point is a small village on the Moreton Bay side of the island. Quandamooka people know it as Pulan.

About the Author

Madeleine Onraet writes poetry that focuses on the spiritual nature of existence, family life and the natural world. Madeleine has a Bachelor of Arts degree from The University of Queensland and was a print journalist. She has worked as a chaplain in Brisbane hospitals. Madeleine lives in Brisbane with her husband, Steve. They are blessed with two sons.

www.ingramcontent.com/pod-product-compliance
Lightning Source LLC
Chambersburg PA
CBHW021837020426
42334CB00014B/664